TeacherTools

CHAPITRE 8

GLENCOE FRENCH 1

Bon voyage!

Conrad J. Schmitt
Katia Brillié Lutz

McGraw Hill **Glencoe**

New York, New York   Columbus, Ohio   Chicago, Illinois   Peoria, Illinois   Woodland Hills, California

Glencoe

The *McGraw-Hill* Companies

Send all inquiries to:
Glencoe/McGraw-Hill
8787 Orion Place
Columbus, OH 43240-4027

ISBN: 0-07-865642-7

Printed in the United States of America.

1 2 3 4 5 6 7   009   11 10 09 08 07 06 05 04

Contents

INTRODUCTION

Following is a list of the resources included in this booklet.

Workbook

Workbook activities provide additional written practice for each chapter. The activities appear in the order in which the material is presented in the Student Edition and are labeled *Easy, Average,* and *Challenging* to help you identify the level of difficulty of the material. An autobiography section is included in each chapter for students to demonstrate mastery of their writing skills. You may wish to include the students' autobiography pages as part of a portfolio.

Audio Activities

These activities are recorded by native speakers from various areas of the French-speaking world to enable students to hear and comprehend different accents. The majority of the activities are new to further enable students to master their listening and speaking skills. However, vocabulary, conversations, and some activities from the Student Edition are included.

TPR Storytelling

Four to six frames or scenes depict a story. Students practice speaking as they would in real-life conversations, requiring "Total Physical Response." First, you tell the story while students act it out. Then, students both tell and act out the story. There are many creative ways to use these activities.

Situation Cards

The Situation Cards simulate real-life situations that require students to communicate in French as though they were in a French-speaking country. A primary goal of these cards is to develop communication strategies using the vocabulary and structures students have learned in the chapter. For your convenience, there are also blank cards for students to create their own "situations" with a partner.

Quizzes with Answer Key

Short quizzes assess students on every vocabulary presentation and each structure point. They are intended to be short to check students' acquisition of the material presented. You may wish to create additional quizzes using ExamView® Pro.

Tests with Answer Key

There are four types of tests presented for each chapter: Reading and Writing, Listening Comprehension, Speaking, and Proficiency. There are two Reading and Writing Tests. One is labeled "Form A" and is designed with a difficulty level of *Easy to Average*. The other is labeled "Form B" and is designed with a difficulty level of *Average to Challenging*. Depending on the ability level of your students, you may choose to give them one test or the other. At the end of the Reading and Writing Tests are questions on the chapter's optional readings. You may eliminate this section if you did not present this optional material to your students. The ExamView® Pro is also available if you wish to prepare additional tests.

Performance Assessment

The Performance Assessment Tasks provide efficient alternatives for assessing language performance in the classroom. The time required for these tasks varies from five to forty minutes. They imitate real activities students might encounter in a French-speaking country. The tasks are linked to the goals of the chapter. They test the knowledge and skills students have learned but also allow for creativity and critical thinking. Students complete some tasks individually, other tasks in pairs.

Dear Parent or Guardian,

Your child is studying French! Foreign language study provides many benefits for students in addition to the ability to communicate in another language. Students who study another language improve their first language skills. They become more aware of the world around them and they learn to appreciate diversity.

In Chapter 8, the students will be learning how to:

- check in for a flight
- talk about some services aboard the plane
- talk about more activities
- ask more questions
- talk about people and things as a group
- discuss air travel in France

You can help your child be successful in his or her study of French even if you are not familiar with the language. Here are a few suggestions to help you help your child practice the material in this chapter.

With your child, use the Internet—either at home or at your local public library—to look up the Web site for a French airline, such as Air France, or an airport in a French-speaking country. As you and your child explore the site together, have your child keep a running list of words that appear on the site that he or she has already learned from Chapter 8. Ask your child questions such as which words appear most frequently or which words would be essential to know while traveling to/from a French-speaking country.

Pretend that you and your child are taking a trip to a French-speaking country. Your child will act as your interpreter for the duration of the trip. Together, write up a quick reference list of questions your child will need to ask airport and airline personnel in order to ensure that you both reach your final destination.

Feel free to plan other activities you think will help your child develop his or her language skills. Thank you for supporting our classroom work. Feel free to contact me if you wish to discuss your child's language education.

Sincerely,

French Teacher

CHAPITRE
8

L'aéroport et l'avion

CHAPITRE 8

L'aéroport et l'avion

Vocabulaire [Mots 1]

1 **À l'aéroport** Identify each illustration. *(Easy)*

1. ___un passeport___ 2. ___un billet___ 3. ___une valise___

4. ___un avion___ 5. ___un comptoir / un hall___ 6. ___le contrôle de sécurité___

2 **Quel est le mot?** Write another word or expression for each phrase below. *(Easy to Average)*

1. un vol qui arrive de Paris ___un vol en provenance de Paris___

2. un vol qui va à Paris ___un vol à destination de Paris___

3. un vol qui commence et finit dans le même pays ___un vol intérieur___

4. un vol qui commence dans un pays et finit dans un autre pays

   ___un vol international___

3 **Moi** Give personal answers. *(Easy to Average)*

1. Tu prends souvent l'avion?

   ___*Answers will vary.*___

2. Tu fais enregistrer tes bagages ou tu prends tout avec toi?

   _____

3. Tu préfères une place côté couloir ou côté fenêtre?

   _____

Vocabulaire **Mots 2**

4 **À bord** Identify each illustration. *(Easy)*

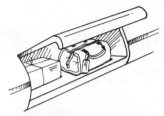

1. ___un siège___   2. ___une hôtesse de l'air___   3. ___un coffre à bagages___

4. ___une ceinture de sécurité___   5. ___un steward___   6. ___un plateau___

5 **Vrai ou faux?** Indicate whether each statement is true (**vrai**) or false (**faux**). *(Easy)*

	vrai	faux
1. Avant de monter en avion, on passe par le contrôle de sécurité.	✔	
2. On sert un repas pendant un vol transatlantique.	✔	
3. On ramasse les plateaux après le repas.	✔	
4. Le pilote sert les repas.		✔
5. Il faut mettre ses bagages dans le couloir.		✔

6 **Quel verbe?** Choose the correct verb to complete each phrase. *(Easy to Average)*

passer   enregistrer   sortir   remplir   servir   choisir   attacher

1. _____choisir_____ une place côté couloir
2. _____passer_____ par le contrôle de sécurité
3. _____sortir_____ les bagages du coffre
4. _____remplir_____ une carte de débarquement
5. _____enregistrer_____ les bagages
6. _____servir_____ un repas
7. _____attacher_____ sa ceinture de sécurité

Structure Les verbes en -ir au présent

7 **Un voyage en avion** Complete with the indicated verb. *(Easy to Average)*

1. Romain et Christophe ____**choisissent**____ un vol Air France. (choisir)

2. Quand Romain fait enregistrer ses bagages, il ____**choisit**____ aussi sa place. (choisir)

3. Pendant le voyage, les deux garçons ont faim. Ils ____**finissent**____ tout leur repas. (finir)

4. Après, ils ____**remplissent**____ leur carte de débarquement. (remplir)

5. Leur avion ____**atterrit**____ à New York à 2 h 45. (atterrir)

8 **Au pluriel** Rewrite each sentence in the plural. *(Average)*

1. Je choisis toujours un vol pendant la journée.

   Nous choisissons toujours un vol pendant la journée.

2. Le passager remplit sa carte de débarquement.

   Les passagers remplissent leur carte de débarquement.

3. L'avion atterrit à l'heure.

   Les avions atterrissent à l'heure.

4. Tu choisis toujours une place côté couloir?

   Vous choisissez toujours une place côté couloir?

5. Elle ne finit pas son repas.

   Elles ne finissent pas leur repas.

9 **Quel nom?** Match the verbs in the left column with the nouns in the right column. *(Easy)*

1. __c__ finir   **a.** le remplissage

2. __e__ choisir   **b.** un atterrissage

3. __a__ remplir   **c.** la fin

4. __b__ atterrir   **d.** une croyance

5. __f__ voir   **e.** un choix

6. __d__ croire   **f.** la vue

Quel et tout

 10 **Céline et Aimé sortent.** Our friends don't know what to wear! Complete each blank with the correct form of **quel** followed by the item of clothing shown in the illustration. *(Easy to Average)*

 1. 2. 3.  4. 5.

1. _____ **Quelle jupe?** _____   4. _____ **Quelles chaussures?** _____

2. _____ **Quel chemisier?** _____   5. _____ **Quel manteau?** _____

3. _____ **Quel pull?** _____

 6.  7. 8. 9. 10.

6. _____ **Quelle chemise?** _____   9. _____ **Quels baskets?** _____

7. _____ **Quel pantalon?** _____   10. _____ **Quelle veste?** _____

8. _____ **Quel anorak?** _____

11 **Tout l'avion** Complete with the appropriate form of **tout** and a definite article. *(Easy to Average)*

1. _____ **Toute la** _____ cabine est non-fumeurs.

2. _____ **Tout le** _____ personnel de bord est français.

3. _____ **Tous les** _____ stewards sont très sympas.

4. _____ **Toutes les** _____ hôtesses de l'air sont sympas.

5. _____ **Toutes les** _____ places sont occupées.

6. _____ **Tous les** _____ bagages sont dans les coffres.

Les verbes **sortir, partir, dormir** et **servir**

12 **En voyage** Rewrite each sentence in the singular. *(Average)*

1. Les passagers partent pour Montréal.

   Le passager part pour Montréal.

2. Nous partons pour l'aéroport à sept heures.

   Je pars pour l'aéroport à sept heures.

3. Pendant le vol, les stewards servent des boissons.

   Pendant le vol, le steward sert des boissons.

4. Les passagers ne dorment pas.

   Le passager ne dort pas.

5. Et vous, vous dormez quand le vol est long?

   Et toi, tu dors quand le vol est long?

6. Vous sortez vos bagages du coffre? Pourquoi?

   Tu sors tes bagages du coffre? Pourquoi?

13 **Quand vous sortez...** Give personal answers. *(Average)*

1. Vous sortez pendant la semaine? Quel(s) jour(s)?

   Answers will vary.

2. Vous sortez pendant le week-end? Quel(s) jour(s)?

   _____

3. Quand vous sortez, vous sortez avec qui?

   _____

Les noms et adjectifs en **-al**

14 **Au pluriel** Rewrite in the plural. *(Easy to Average)*

1. un vol international **des vols internationaux**

2. un journal **des journaux**

3. une organisation internationale **des organisations internationales**

4. la ville principale **les villes principales**

5. un parc municipale **des parcs municipaux**

Un peu plus

A **Carte de débarquement** Fill out the following disembarkation card. Use the boarding pass to fill out #7. (*Easy to Average*)

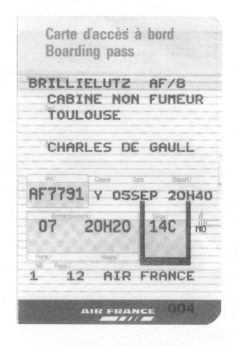

B **Facile à comprendre!** You have already seen that French shares a lot of vocabulary with the other Romance languages derived from Latin. Look at the expressions below in Spanish, Italian, and Portuguese and notice how much you could understand at an airport in Madrid, Mexico City, Rome, Lisbon, or Rio de Janeiro. (*Easy*)

français	espagnol	italien	portugais
la ligne aérienne	la línea aérea	la linea aerea	a linha aerea
le vol	el vuelo	il volo	o vôo
le passeport	el pasaporte	il passaporto	o passaporte
la porte	la puerta	la porta	a porta
la carte d'embarquement	la tarjeta de embarque	la carta d'imbarco	a cartão de embarque
la douane	la aduana	la dogana	a alfândega
la destination	el destino	la destinazione	o destino
le billet	el billete	il biglietto	o bilhete
le passager	el pasajero	il passaggero	o passageiro
le voyage	el viaje	il viaggio	a viagem

Nom _____ Date _____

 À l'aéroport Charles-de-Gaulle If you have a connecting flight, you often have to transfer to another location in the airport. Here is a map of Terminal 2 at Charles-de-Gaulle Airport. Study it and answer the following questions. Make sure you estimate the distances correctly. *(Average)*

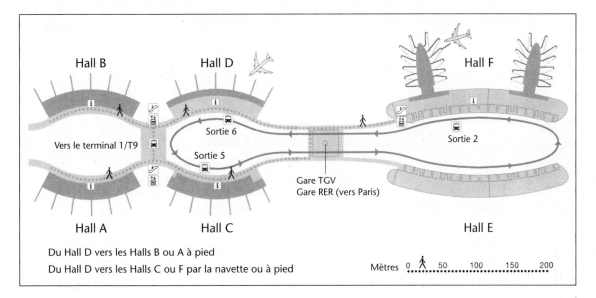

1. Quelle est la distance entre le hall F et le hall D?

   À peu près 400 mètres.

2. Et quelle est la distance entre le hall D et le hall B?

   À peu près 200 mètres.

3. Vous arrivez dans le hall F. Vous avez beaucoup de bagages. Votre vol de correspondance part du hall B. Qu'est-ce que vous allez faire? Vous allez trouver un chariot et y aller à pied ou vous allez prendre la navette? Où allez-vous prendre la navette? Jusqu'où?

   Answers will vary.

   _____

   _____

   _____

Mon autobiographie

Do you like to travel? Do you travel often? Do you travel by plane? If you do, tell about your experiences.

If you don't travel by plane, imagine a trip that you would like to take. Tell something about the airport near your home and something about the flight you are going to take. Include as many details as you can.

Mon autobiographie

CHAPITRE 8

L'aéroport et l'avion

L'aéroport et l'avion

Première partie

Vocabulaire Mots 1

Activité 1 Listen and repeat.

(Textbook, pages 260–261)
(CD 5, Track 16)
(Workbook and Audio Activities, page A39)

Repeat after the speaker.

À l'aéroport
le hall de l'aérogare
un agent
le comptoir de la compagnie aérienne

Maintenant Justine est dans le hall de l'aéroport.
Elle fait enregistrer ses bagages.
L'agent vérifie son billet.

Justine choisit une place dans l'avion.
Elle demande une place côté couloir.

une passagère
un bagage à main
une valise

les arrivées
le numéro du vol
un écran

L'avion a du retard.
L'avion n'est pas à l'heure.

une carte d'embarquement
un billet
un passeport

passer par le contrôle de sécurité
la porte d'embarquement
le départ

L'avion part de la porte 32.

L'avion atterrit.

la piste
L'avion décolle.

Justine aime voyager.
Elle fait un voyage à Montréal.
Avant le voyage elle fait sa valise.

un vol à destination de Paris, c'est un vol qui va à Paris
un vol en provenance de Lyon, c'est un vol qui arrive de Lyon
un vol intérieur, c'est un vol entre deux villes du même pays (Paris–Lyon)
un vol international, c'est un vol entre deux villes de pays différents (Paris–Rome)

Activité 2 Listen and choose.

(CD 5, Track 17)
(Workbook and Audio Activities, page A39)

Look at the illustrations on your activity sheet. You will hear a series of statements about Marguerite's plane trip. Write the number of the statement under the corresponding illustration.

1. Marguerite fait un voyage. D'abord elle fait ses valises.
2. Elle a beaucoup de valises.
3. Elle fait enregistrer ses bagages.
4. Elle regarde l'écran.
5. Elle donne son billet.
6. Elle choisit une place côté couloir.
7. L'avion décolle.
8. L'avion atterrit.

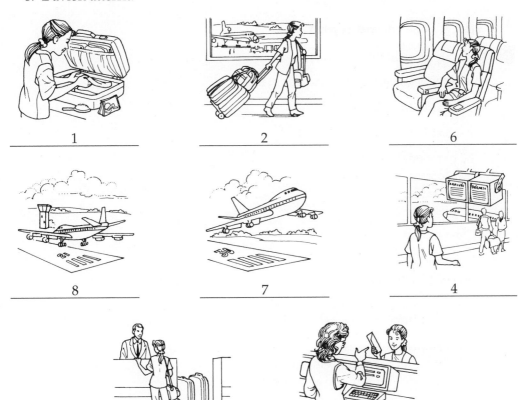

1

2

6

8

7

4

3

5

Activité 3 Listen and choose.

(CD 5, Track 18)
(Workbook and Audio Activities, page A39)

For each statement you hear, decide if the person is most likely talking about a domestic flight, an international flight, or both, and check the appropriate box.

1. On achète les billets maintenant?
2. Vérifiez bien que vous avez votre passeport.
3. Tout le monde passe au contrôle de sécurité.
4. Mais quand est-ce que vous allez faire vos valises?
5. Vous voulez un repas spécial?
6. Ah non, pour les vols internationaux, ce n'est pas ici.
7. J'ai des bagages à main. C'est tout.
8. J'ai beaucoup de valises parce que je vais dans quatre pays différents.

	1.	2.	3.	4.	5.	6.	7.	8.
un vol intérieur							✔	
un vol international		✔				✔		✔
les deux	✔		✔	✔	✔			

Vocabulaire Mots 2

Activité 4 Listen and repeat.

(Textbook, pages 264–265)
(CD 5, Track 19)
(Workbook and Audio Activities, page A40)

Repeat after the speaker.

À bord

Le personnel de bord
le pilote
le steward
l'hôtesse de l'air

C'est un vol non-fumeurs.

la cabine
un coffre à bagages
un siège

Il faut mettre vos bagages sous le siège devant vous ou dans le coffre à bagages.

une ceinture de sécurité
—Il faut attacher votre ceinture de sécurité.
L'hôtesse de l'air fait une annonce.

Le steward sert des boissons à bord.
On sert un repas.

—Vous ne finissez pas votre repas?
—Non, merci. Je n'ai plus faim.
On ramasse les plateaux.

Un passager sort ses bagages du coffre à bagages.
Une passagère dort.
Une autre remplit sa carte de débarquement.

Activité 5 Listen and choose.
(CD 5, Track 20)
(Workbook and Audio Activities, page A40)

Write the number of each word you hear next to its opposite.

1. l'arrivée
2. l'embarquement
3. décoller
4. intérieur
5. en provenance de

à destination de	5
international	4
le débarquement	2
le départ	1
atterrir	3

Activité 6 Listen and choose.
(CD 5, Track 21)
(Workbook and Audio Activities, page A40)

You will hear a series of statements. Decide if they are being said before the flight, during the flight, or after the flight, and check the appropriate box.

1. Je voudrais une place côté couloir, s'il vous plaît.
2. Je vais faire mes valises dans une demi-heure.
3. Remplissez vos cartes de débarquement, s'il vous plaît.
4. Par ici pour le contrôle de sécurité, s'il vous plaît.
5. Vous avez combien de valises?
6. On va atterrir dans vingt minutes.
7. Votre billet et votre passeport, s'il vous plaît.

	1.	2.	3.	4.	5.	6.	7.
avant le vol	✔	✔		✔	✔		✔
pendant le vol			✔			✔	
après le vol							

Structure

Activité 7 Listen and answer.

(CD 5, Track 22)
(Workbook and Audio Activities, page A40)

As you have noticed, most French verbs, whether they are regular or irregular, sound alike in the singular: **j'aime, tu aimes, il aime; je fais, tu fais, il fait.** This is also true for verbs ending in **-ir.** Respond to the statements according to the model.

Modèle: Quand Marie fait un voyage, elle choisit Air France.
Moi aussi, je choisis Air France.

Ready? Begin.

1. Quand Marie fait un voyage, elle choisit Air France.
(Moi aussi, je choisis Air France.)
2. Elle choisit une place non-fumeurs.
(Moi aussi, je choisis une place non-fumeurs.)
3. Elle remplit sa carte de débarquement.
(Moi aussi, je remplis ma carte de débarquement.)
4. Elle atterrit à Charles-de-Gaulle.
(Moi aussi, j'atterris à Charles-de-Gaulle.)

Activité 8 Listen and choose.

(CD 5, Track 23)
(Workbook and Audio Activities, page A40)

As you know, in French, you often cannot tell the difference between singular **il** or **elle** and plural **ils** or **elles,** but the verb form will give you a clue. Decide whether the following statements refer to **Hugo, Hugo et son frère, Ève,** or **Ève et Amélie.**

1. Ils partent demain.
2. Elle dort encore.
3. Il ne sort pas assez.
4. Elles finissent toujours avant les autres.
5. Ils servent le dîner.
6. Elle choisit toujours une place côté couloir.
7. Il remplit sa carte de débarquement.
8. Ils dorment dix heures par jour!

	1.	2.	3.	4.	5.	6.	7.	8.
Hugo			✔				✔	
Hugo et son frère	✔				✔			✔
Ève		✔				✔		
Ève et Amélie				✔				

Audio Activities, Teacher Edition
Copyright © by The McGraw-Hill Companies, Inc.

Activité 9 Listen.

(Textbook, page 273)
(CD 5, Track 24)
(Workbook and Audio Activities, page A40)

You will hear a conversation between Valérie and Philippe. Just listen.

Valérie: Demain, on part pour Tunis, Marie et moi!
Philippe: Vous partez à quelle heure?
Valérie: On part à onze heures.
Philippe: Et vous partez de quel aéroport?
Valérie: D'Orly. C'est la première fois que je pars d'Orly.
Philippe: Ah oui?
Valérie: Oui, en général, nous partons toujours de Charles-de-Gaulle.

Activité 10 Listen and repeat.

(CD 5, Track 24)
(Workbook and Audio Activities, page A40)

Now repeat each line of the conversation after the speaker.

Valérie: Demain, on part pour Tunis, Marie et moi!
Philippe: Vous partez à quelle heure?
Valérie: On part à onze heures.
Philippe: Et vous partez de quel aéroport?
Valérie: D'Orly. C'est la première fois que je pars d'Orly.
Philippe: Ah oui?
Valérie: Oui, en général, nous partons toujours de Charles-de-Gaulle.

Activité 11 Listen and perform!

(CD 5, Track 24)
(Workbook and Audio Activities, page A41)

Now you will play the part of Philippe. Try to remember what Philippe said and play his part. Good luck!

Valérie: **Demain, on part pour Tunis, Marie et moi!**

Philippe: Vous partez à quelle heure? _____

Valérie: **On part à onze heures.**

Philippe: Et vous partez de quel aéroport? _____

Valérie: **D'Orly. C'est la première fois que je pars d'Orly.**

Philippe: Ah oui? _____

Valérie: **Oui, en général, nous partons toujours de Charles-de-Gaulle.**

Activité 12 Listen and choose.

(CD 5, Track 25)
(Workbook and Audio Activities, page A41)

You have already seen how a liaison can be a number cue: **il arrive** is about one person, **ils arrivent** is about several people. The same is true with **quel** when it is followed by a vowel. When it's followed by a consonant, you have to listen for some other cues. Let's see if you can decide if the speaker is talking about one or several people or things. Check the appropriate box.

1. Tu pars avec quels amis?
2. C'est quel vol international?
3. Quels journaux tu achètes le matin?
4. Tu veux parler à quel agent?
5. Tu vas à quel hôtel à Paris?
6. Tu veux être à côté de quels élèves?
7. Quel plat principal tu vas commander?
8. Quelles hôtesses?

	1.	2.	3.	4.	5.	6.	7.	8.
un(e)		✔		✔	✔		✔	
deux ou plus	✔		✔			✔		✔

Conversation   Dans le hall des départs

Activité A Listen.

(Textbook, page 276)
(CD 5, Track 26)
(Workbook and Audio Activities, page A41)

You will hear a conversation between Cécile and Pierre. Listen.

> Départ à destination de Toulouse, vol Air France numéro 6106. Embarquement immédiat, porte 24.

Cécile: C'est notre vol. On y va?
Pierre: D'accord. Tu sors les cartes d'embarquement?
Cécile: Mais moi, je n'ai pas les cartes d'embarquement!
Pierre: Tu n'as pas les cartes d'embarquement! Ben, elles sont où alors?
Cécile: Dans ton sac?
Pierre: Ah, oui. Les voilà! On part de la porte 24.
Cécile: On a quelles places?
Pierre: 10A et 10B.
Cécile: Ah, c'est bien. C'est à l'avant de la cabine. On va pouvoir sortir vite.

Activité B Listen and choose.

(CD 5, Track 26)
(Workbook and Audio Activities, page A41)

You will now hear the conversation a second time. After that, you will hear some statements about the conversation and you will have to determine whether they are true or false.

> Départ à destination de Toulouse, vol Air France numéro 6106. Embarquement immédiat, porte 24.

Cécile: C'est notre vol. On y va?
Pierre: D'accord. Tu sors les cartes d'embarquement?
Cécile: Mais moi, je n'ai pas les cartes d'embarquement!
Pierre: Tu n'as pas les cartes d'embarquement! Ben, elles sont où alors?
Cécile: Dans ton sac?
Pierre: Ah, oui. Les voilà! On part de la porte 24.
Cécile: On a quelles places?
Pierre: 10A et 10B.
Cécile: Ah, c'est bien. C'est à l'avant de la cabine. On va pouvoir sortir vite.

Now check **vrai** or **faux.**

1. Cécile et Pierre sont à l'aéroport.
2. On annonce l'embarquement de leur vol.
3. C'est Pierre qui a les cartes d'embarquement.
4. Les cartes d'embarquement sont dans le sac de Pierre.
5. Ils partent de la porte 24.
6. Ils ont des places à l'avant de l'avion.

	1.	2.	3.	4.	5.	6.
vrai	✔	✔	✔	✔	✔	✔
faux						

Prononciation Le son /l/ final

Activité A Listen and repeat.

(Textbook, page 277)
(CD 5, Track 27)
(Workbook and Audio Activities, page A41)

The names Michelle and Nicole are originally French names, but today many American girls also have these names. When you hear French people say Michelle and Nicole, the final /l/ sound is much softer than in English. Listen to the difference: Michelle *(American)*—**Michelle** *(French)*, Nicole *(American)*—**Nicole** *(French).*

Now repeat the following words.

il	vol	animal	elle	école
salle	décolle	journal	quel	ville

Now repeat the following sentences.

C'est un vol international spécial.
Quelle est la ville principale?
Mademoiselle Michelle, elle est très belle.

Lettres et sons Les consonnes finales c, r, f et l

Activité B Listen, read, and repeat.
(CD 5, Track 27)
(Workbook and Audio Activities, page A41)

You have seen that final consonants are usually not pronounced in French. However, in short, mostly one-syllable words, **c, r, f,** and **l** are usually pronounced. An easy way to remember is to think of the consonants in the English word CaReFuL.

Listen and repeat. Follow along on your activity sheet.

> **le sac**
>
> **le jour   la cour   le soir   cher**
>
> **neuf   soif   le bœuf   l'œuf**
>
> **quel   le vol   avril**

Activité C Listen and write.
(CD 5, Track 27)
(Workbook and Audio Activities, page A42)

Fill in the blanks as you listen to the speaker.

> —Tu pars par quel vol?
> —Le vol trois cent neuf, ce soir.
> —Moi, je préfère les vols de jour.
> —Moi pas. Je dors. Et ce n'est pas cher.

—**Tu pars par** ___quel___ ___vol___ **?**

—**Le vol trois cent** ___neuf___ **, ce** ___soir___ **.**

—**Moi, je préfère les vols de** ___jour___ **.**

—**Moi pas. Je dors. Et ce n'est pas** ___cher___ **.**

Lecture culturelle On va en France.

Activité A Read and listen.

(Textbook, pages 278–279)
(CD 5, Track 28)
(Workbook and Audio Activities, page A42)

You will hear about a group of American kids taking a trip to France with their French teacher. But first, read the statements printed on your answer sheet. After the reading, you will be asked whether they are true or false. *(pause)*

1. **La classe de Mme Cadet va en France au mois de juillet.**
2. **Ils prennent un vol Air France.**
3. **Tous les élèves de Mme Cadet dorment pendant le vol.**
4. **Ils ne vont pas aller à Paris.**
5. **Leur avion atterrit à l'aéroport Charles-de-Gaulle.**
6. **De l'aéroport, ils prennent le métro pour aller à Paris.**

Ready? OK, begin.

C'est le mois d'avril et toute la classe de Madame Cadet va passer les vacances de Pâques en France. Ils sont maintenant dans le hall de l'aérogare 1 de l'aéroport international JFK à New York. Ils sont au comptoir d'Air France. Ils vont prendre le vol 007. L'agent vérifie leurs billets et leurs passeports. Il donne toutes les cartes d'embarquement à Madame Cadet.

Les élèves passent par le contrôle de sécurité. Leur avion part de la porte A. Il part à l'heure. Il ne va pas avoir de retard. Après le décollage, le personnel de bord sert des boissons et un repas. Après le repas, il y a un film. Beaucoup de personnes ne regardent pas le film, elles dorment. Mais pas les élèves de Madame Cadet. Ils ne dorment pas. Ils parlent de leur voyage. Ils vont passer quelques jours à Paris et ensuite ils vont en Normandie. Là, ils vont visiter le Mont-Saint-Michel. Avant l'arrivée à Paris, tout le monde remplit une carte de débarquement.

À huit heures du matin, après un vol agréable, l'avion atterrit à l'aéroport Charles-de-Gaulle à Roissy. Charles-de-Gaulle est un des deux aéroports de Paris. D'abord, il faut passer au contrôle des passeports. Ensuite les formalités de douane sont très simples et quarante minutes après l'atterrissage, les élèves de Madame Cadet sont dans l'autocar (le bus) qui fait la navette entre Paris et l'aéroport. Tout le monde est très fatigué après le long vol. Vous croyez qu'ils vont dormir? Pas question! Le premier jour à Paris, on ne dort pas. On va visiter la belle ville de Paris.

Activité B Read and choose.
(CD 5, Track 28)
(Workbook and Audio Activities, page A42)

Now read the statements again. Check **vrai** or **faux** according to what you heard in the reading.

1. **La classe de Mme Cadet va en France au mois de juillet.**
2. **Ils prennent un vol Air France.**
3. **Tous les élèves de Mme Cadet dorment pendant le vol.**
4. **Ils ne vont pas aller à Paris.**
5. **Leur avion atterrit à l'aéroport Charles-de-Gaulle.**
6. **De l'aéroport, ils prennent le métro pour aller à Paris.**

	1.	2.	3.	4.	5.	6.
vrai		✔			✔	
faux	✔		✔	✔		✔

Deuxième partie

Activité A Listen and fill in.

(CD 5, Track 29)

(Workbook and Audio Activities, page A43)

Mlle Dupré is organizing a trip for her boss. Listen to her conversation with the travel agent, and fill in the information in the chart as you listen. First, take a moment to look over the chart.

Ready? Let's go!

L'agent:	Air France, bonjour.
Mlle Dupré:	Bonjour, monsieur. Je voudrais faire des réservations pour la semaine prochaine.
L'agent:	Oui. Départ de Paris?
Mlle Dupré:	Oui. Alors d'abord Paris-Bordeaux, puis Bordeaux-Marseille, puis Marseille-Lyon et finalement, Lyon-Paris.
L'agent:	Pour quels jours?
Mlle Dupré:	Alors départ de Paris le 13, le 13 juillet. Le matin si possible.
L'agent:	Oui. J'ai le vol 43 qui part d'Orly-Ouest à 10 h 30 et qui arrive à Bordeaux à 11 h 35.
Mlle Dupré:	Bien. Maintenant pour le 15, attendez… départ de Bordeaux en fin d'après-midi. Vers 17 h 30.
L'agent:	Oui, départ à 18 h et arrivée à Marseille à 18 h 40, ça vous va?
Mlle Dupré:	Euh, oui. C'est quel vol?
L'agent:	Le vol 15.
Mlle Dupré:	Parfait. Et maintenant, Marseille-Lyon, le 18 juillet. Le matin.
L'agent:	8 h 50?
Mlle Dupré:	C'est un peu tôt.
L'agent:	Alors 9 h 35?
Mlle Dupré:	Oui. Et finalement le retour sur Paris pour le 22 au soir.
L'agent:	Eh bien, départ de Lyon à 20 h 10 et arrivée à Orly-Sud à 21 h 15.
Mlle Dupré:	Très bien. Alors c'est au nom de Gagné, Marc Gagné.

	Jour	N° de vol	Heure de départ	Heure d'arrivée
PARIS-BORDEAUX	13	43	10 h 30	11 h 35
BORDEAUX-MARSEILLE	15	15	18 h	18 h 40
MARSEILLE-LYON	18	—	9 h 35	—
LYON-PARIS	22	—	20 h 10	21 h 15

Activité B Listen and answer.

(CD 5, Track 30)
(Workbook and Audio Activities, page A43)

Look at the map of the time zones on your activity sheet. Answer the questions getting the information needed from the map. Use **du matin, de l'après-midi,** and **du soir** in your answer.

1. Quand il est une heure du matin à Paris, il est quelle heure à New York?
   (Il est sept heures du soir.)
2. Et à Québec?
   (Il est sept heures du soir aussi.)
3. Et à Fort-de-France?
   (Il est huit heures du soir.)
4. Et à Dakar?
   (Il est minuit.)
5. Et à San Francisco?
   (Il est quatre heures de l'après-midi.)
6. Et à Alger?
   (Il est une heure du matin.)

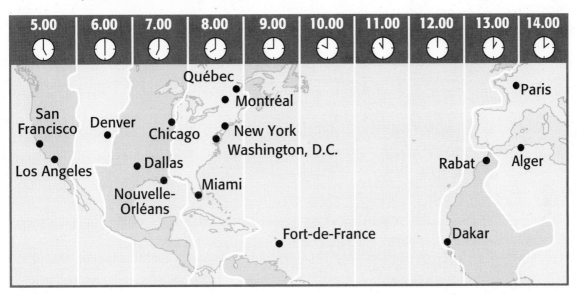

Fin du Chapitre 8

L'aéroport et l'avion

INTRODUCTION

Much of real-life conversation is telling short stories: what you did last night, what happened to you, what movie you saw last week, etc. Conversations can be animated with gestures. The same incident is told and retold but never in exactly the same way.

TPR Storytelling is a way of learning natural speech patterns as they would occur in real-life conversations. These stories require *TPR—Total Physical Response.* They are divided into four to six frames or scenes, which will be first told by the teacher and acted out by students and then told by all students.

To begin, you need to have ready any props necessary to help tell the story. You must also have practiced the story beforehand to be well prepared; however, it is recommended that you not memorize it. Be flexible, retelling it in a slightly different manner each time, just like in real life. Use volunteer students to be your actors. You may wish to select them a day in advance and give them an idea of what will be expected. Start telling the story and model what you want the students to do. You may want to whisper instructions to them or suggest gestures or poses to them. If in the story you say **Jean dit: Je n'ai pas d'argent,** prompt the actor playing Jean to say **Je n'ai pas d'argent** as you encourage him to pull out his empty pockets. Move the students to a different spot in the room if the action in the story requires a change of scene. Always use volunteers; don't embarrass shy students.

Go through the story a second time, stopping after each short section to ask the questions. The whole class may want to shout out the answers, or you can just ask individuals to answer. The question format is very important to reinforce the story and also to allow students to start uttering parts of the story in French. After doing one frame, go on to the next frame immediately or pause to either have individuals tell that frame or have partners practice that frame with each other. After you have done all the frames in this manner, show the art on an overhead projector. (Note: You may wish to convert the art pages in this booklet to overhead transparencies. The latter is accomplished by placing a blank acetate in the paper tray of your photocopy machine, then proceeding to make a copy of your Blackline Master, as though you were making a paper copy.) Have pairs or individuals retell the story; you may prefer to have small groups of speakers and actors practice the whole story while you circulate and listen. Later you may wish to select individuals to perform and tell it all.

As possible follow-up assignments, you may wish to:
- copy the story and questions for students to read and answer
- copy the story with words or phrases missing to be filled in by students
- write a similar story and ask students to illustrate it
- number several sentences from the story and have students match them to the pictures
- copy the pictures and have students write the sentences about each one.

Stories involve listening and speaking, and then later, reading and writing. The communicative value of TPR Storytelling is as great as you wish to make it.

L'aéroport et l'avion

Frame 1 Claudine et Nadine Lascaux sont des lycéennes en vacances. Elles vont faire un voyage. Elles sont dans le hall de l'aéroport Orly, près de Paris, avec des bagages à main et deux petites valises. Elles regardent l'écran des vols. Claudine <u>dit</u>: «Bon! L'avion est à l'heure.» Nadine dit: «Oui, on part de la porte 3. Mais il faut faire enregistrer nos bagages. Allons-y!»

Qui sont Claudine et Nadine Lascaux? Elles vont faire un voyage? Elles sont où? Elles ont combien de valises? Qu'est-ce qu'elles regardent? Leur avion a du retard? Le vol part de quelle porte?

Frame 2 Colin et Martin Senghor sont à l'aéroport aussi. Ils ont de grands sacs à dos et parlent avec un agent au comptoir de la compagnie aérienne Alamérica. L'agent demande: «Vous choisissez côté couloir ou côté fenêtre?» Colin dit: «Côté couloir, s'il vous plaît, madame. Mon frère préfère côté fenêtre.» L'agent dit: «Voilà vos cartes d'embarquement. Bon voyage!»

Où sont Martin et Colin? Ils ont des sacs à dos? Ils parlent avec qui? Quel est le nom de la compagnie aérienne? Colin choisit une place côté couloir ou côté fenêtre? Son frère préfère côté fenêtre?

Frame 3 Martin voit Nadine et Claudine. Il dit à son frère: «Voilà les sœurs Lascaux! Elles voyagent aussi!» Nadine dit: «Bonjour, Colin, bonjour, Martin. Quelle coïncidence! Vous allez où?» Martin dit: «Nous allons à Montréal.» Nadine dit: «Montréal, c'est très beau. Mais le vol est très long!» Colin dit: «On aime voyager et prendre l'avion. Les stewards et les hôtesses de l'air servent des boissons et le dîner. On regarde un film et ensuite, on dort. C'est sympa!» Martin dit: «Moi, je vais dormir pendant tout le vol!» Claudine dit: «Ah, voilà un agent libre! Allons-y, Nadine!» *(Les sœurs font enregistrer leurs valises.)*

Où vont Martin et Colin? C'est un vol intérieur ou international? Colin et Martin détestent voyager? Qui sert des boissons? Ils servent le dîner aussi? Martin va regarder le film? Il va dormir pendant tout le vol? L'agent est libre ou occupée?

Frame 4 Il y a une annonce: «Attention, voyageurs! Vols internationaux Alamérica, numéro 25 et numéro 33, partent dans vingt minutes.» Martin regarde sa carte d'embarquement. Il dit: «Oh là là, vol 25, c'est nous!» Claudine dit: «Et vol 33, c'est nous! <u>Amusez-vous bien</u> à Montréal!» «Et vous, vous allez où?» demande Colin. «Nous allons voir nos cousins à Paris!» dit Nadine. «À Paris? Tu rigoles? Nous sommes à Paris!» dit Colin. Claudine dit: «Oui, mais nos cousins habitent à Paris, Texas! Au revoir, Martin, Colin! Bon voyage!»

Les vols partent dans combien de minutes? Ce sont des vols internationaux? Où habitent les cousins de Claudine et de Nadine? Nadine rigole? Les sœurs vont aux États-Unis? Qu'est-ce qu'on dit aux amis quand ils font un voyage?

1   **Aéroport Orly**

CHAPITRE 8

L'aéroport et l'avion

INTRODUCTION

Rationale

The Situation Cards, as their name implies, simulate real-life situations that require students to communicate in French, exactly as though they were in a French-speaking country. The Situation Cards operate on the assumption that the person to whom the message is to be conveyed understands no English. Therefore, students must focus on producing the French vocabulary and structures necessary to negotiate the situations successfully. This will often entail a certain degree of creativity, which is to be encouraged since a primary goal of the Situation Cards is to foster the development of communication strategies: paraphrasing, inventing circumlocutions, asking for help from the "native speaker," using gestures, etc.

Description

The Situation Cards are available in Blackline Master form for ease of duplication. In preparing the cards for student use, we suggest you photocopy as many sets as necessary, keeping the original set intact. Cut the photocopied sets into their individual cards. For longer durability and protection, you may wish to laminate the cards prior to distribution. For storage, you may wish to keep all cards for each chapter in an appropriately marked envelope.

The Situation Cards are keyed to every chapter in **Bon voyage!** and will serve as a means of strengthening your students' oral mastery of the vocabulary and grammar, chapter by chapter. There are four situations for each chapter, organized from A to D in order of increasing difficulty. Each situation is printed in English and focuses on a specific task. There are always at least two people involved in the situation. Although these situations are not paired activities strictly speaking, it is recommended that the teacher play the role of the "native speaker" interlocutor. Many of the easier situations will require little interaction. To negotiate the situation the student might only need to ask a simple question of the "native speaker." For example, Situation Card A, Chapter 2, reads: "You are walking down the street in Toulouse, on your way to the movies. You see your French teacher. Greet him or her." The student must say, **Bonjour madame (monsieur)**. The teacher may of course reply, **Très bien**, in order to lend authenticity to the situation. But no further response on the part of the student is necessary.

A greater degree of dialogue will occasionally be elicited by the more difficult situations. Situation Card D, Chapter 7, for example, asks the student to return an article of clothing to a store where it was purchased and explain to the salesperson what the problem with the item is. Clearly, the complexity of the interaction in this situation will depend not only on the student's oral mastery of French, but also to some extent on the imagination and creativity of both student and teacher. In this respect, the Situation Cards can be the catalyst for pleasurable language-learning experiences to which students may look forward after completing any given chapter in their textbooks.

Suggestions for Using the Situation Cards

Select an appropriate Situation Card and hand it to the student. Allow the student to read the card, and when he or she is ready, the "situation" begins. The teacher should begin by greeting the student or giving a simple cue, depending on the situation. For example, **Bonjour. Vous désirez?** will suffice for a situation involving a restaurant or a store, where the teacher must play the part of a server or salesperson. The student "understands" that you, in your role as native French speaker, know no English. It is recommended that you act friendly and interested at all times and provide any help a native speaker would provide. Do not, however, correct any student errors during the situation. It is important to allow for spontaneity and creativity during the role-play. The conversation should be interrupted only if the student is not understood. The "native speaker" should ask for clarification or rephrasing as he or she would in real life. To challenge more able students, you may wish to add "complications." When the teacher considers the situation complete, he or she thanks the student and retrieves the card.

If you are fortunate enough to have native French speakers among your students, or extremely able non-native speakers, call on them to serve as the "native speaker" in the situations. Remember, too, that these situations can be supplemented by others of your own or your students' devising.

All situations in the Situation Cards accompanying **Bon voyage**! are at the Novice Level of the ACTFL Oral Proficiency Interview Scale. For more information regarding the relationship between these Situation Cards and the Oral Proficiency Interview, please see the Introduction to the Tests in this TeacherTools Fast File booklet.

B

You're at the airport in Paris and your flight for Guadeloupe leaves in five minutes. You don't know what gate it leaves from. Ask someone.

D

You're at a travel agency in Nice. Tell the travel agent that you'd like to fly to Paris. Then find out what time flights leave for Paris and what time they arrive.

A

You're at the Orly Airport in Paris. You're checking in for a flight to Rome. Tell the ticket agent where you'd like to sit.

C

Your plane from the U.S. has just landed in Paris. You don't know what the procedure is. Ask someone what you do first, go through immigration or get your luggage.

CHAPITRE 8

L'aéroport et l'avion

Quiz 1

Vocabulaire Mots 1

A Complete each sentence with an appropriate word.

1–2. Un agent vérifie les billets et les passeports au _____ de la

compagnie aérienne dans le hall de l'_____.

3–5. Un _____ indique les heures des _____

et des _____ des vols.

6. L'avion n'est pas à l'heure. Il a du _____.

7. Les passagers passent par le _____ de sécurité.

8. L'avion part de la _____ numéro 32.

9–10. Un passager _____ une place dans l'avion. Il préfère une

place _____ couloir.

Nom _____ Date _____

Quiz 2

Vocabulaire  Mots 2

A Identify each item.

   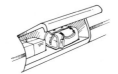   

1. _____ 2. _____ 3. _____

4. _____ 5. _____

B Complete each sentence with an appropriate word.

1. Le steward _____ des boissons et un repas pendant le vol.

2. Un passager _____ ses bagages du coffre à bagages.

3–4. Il faut _____ vos bagages à main sous le

_____ devant vous.

5. Un passager _____ sa carte de débarquement.

Quiz 3

Structure

Les verbes en -ir

A Complete each sentence with the correct form of the indicated verb.

1. Les passagers _____ leurs places dans l'avion. (choisir)

2. L'avion _____ à l'heure. (atterrir)

3. Le steward _____ son travail. (finir)

4. Comme dessert, je _____ une glace. (choisir)

5. Qu'est-ce que vous _____? (choisir)

6. Nous _____ une carte de débarquement. (remplir)

7. Tu _____ tes devoirs. (finir)

8. Ils _____ une place côté couloir. (choisir)

Nom _____ Date _____

8 Quiz 4

Structure

Quel et tout

A Complete each sentence with the correct form of the indicated adjective.

1. _____ les vols sont complets. Il n'y a pas de places. (tout)

2. Tu vas prendre _____ vol? (quel)

3. _____ hôtesses de l'air travaillent pour Air France? (quel)

4. _____ le personnel de bord est très sympa. (tout)

5. _____ les amies de Carole vont faire le voyage avec elle. (tout)

Nom _____ Date _____

Quiz 5

Structure

Les verbes **sortir, partir, dormir** et **servir**

A Complete each sentence with the correct form of the indicated verb.

1. Vous _____ pendant les vols? (dormir)

2. Elles _____ demain. (partir)

3. Je _____ mon billet de mon sac à dos. (sortir)

4. Le steward _____ le dîner à bord. (servir)

5. Tu _____ à quelle heure? (partir)

Answer Key

CHAPITRE 8

Quiz 1: Mots 1

1–2. comptoir, aéroport (aérogare)
3–5. écran, arrivées, départs
   6. retard
   7. contrôle
   8. porte
9–10. choisit, côté

Quiz 2: Mots 2

A

1. un siège
2. un coffre à bagages
3. un repas (une collation)
4. une ceinture de sécurité
5. le personnel de bord

B

1. sert
2. sort
3–4. mettre, siège
   5. remplit

Quiz 3: Les verbes en -ir

1. choisissent
2. atterrit
3. finit
4. choisis
5. choisissez
6. remplissons
7. finis
8. choisissent

Quiz 4: Quel et tout

1. Tous
2. quel
3. Quelles
4. Tout
5. Toutes

Quiz 5: Les verbes sortir, partir, dormir et servir

1. dormez
2. partent
3. sors
4. sert
5. pars

CHAPITRE 8

L'aéroport et l'avion

INTRODUCTION

The Tests for **Bon voyage!** Level 1 include the following components, each designed to measure a specific skill or combination of skills as well as knowledge about French culture.

1. Chapter and Unit Achievement Tests
   - Reading and Writing Tests
   - Listening Comprehension Tests
2. Chapter and Unit Speaking Tests
3. Chapter Proficiency Tests
4. ExamView® Pro (packaged separately)

The Reading and Writing Tests, Listening Comprehension Tests, Speaking Tests, and Proficiency Tests are all included in this TeacherTools booklet.

Achievement vs. Proficiency Tests

A foreign language achievement test evaluates the extent to which a student has mastered the material presented in a chapter, course, or program. A proficiency test assesses a student's ability to use the language in real-life contexts. Following is a more detailed description of both the achievement and proficiency tests accompanying the **Bon voyage!** Level 1 textbook.

Chapter and Unit Achievement Tests

The Chapter Achievement Tests for **Bon voyage!** Level 1 measure vocabulary and grammar concepts via reading, writing, and listening formats. There are two levels of Reading and Writing Tests—*Easy to Average* and *Average to Challenging*. In this way, the teacher can individualize the tests to the students' different ability levels, making it more possible for all students to see positive results. Use the test labeled "Form A" for an easier test. Use the test labeled "Form B" for a more challenging test. In order to test cultural information, a section corresponding to the first **Lecture culturelle** in the Student Textbook is included on each test. After the Form B Test is a test on the optional readings. This can be used with either the Form A Test or the Form B Test. The audio section of each Listening Comprehension Test has been recorded by native French speakers on compact disc. If the teacher chooses to read the test items aloud rather than using the recorded version, the script for the listening tests is included with the Listening Comprehension Answer Key. The Unit Achievement Tests can be administered upon completion of each **Révision** section of the Student Textbook. An Answer Key is provided for both the Reading and Writing Tests and the Listening Comprehension Tests immediately following these tests.

Chapter and Unit Speaking Tests

Day-to-day interaction with students gives teachers a general idea of how each individual is progressing in his or her ability to speak French. The variety of oral activities included in each chapter of the Student Textbook provides ample opportunity for teachers to monitor their students' progress in speaking. The Chapter and Unit Speaking Tests, however, allow teachers to assess the speaking skill more concretely and systematically. Each test includes several conversational topics to which the individual student should respond orally. We recommend that each student speak on two or more of the topics provided in order to give him or her the maximum opportunity to speak. The teacher may wish to add other topics to those provided on the Speaking Test.

When to Administer Speaking Tests

Following are some suggestions for administering a speaking test to each of the students periodically through the year while at the same time attending to the needs of the class as a whole. Perhaps the most practical approach is to schedule in-class reading or writing assignments during those times when the teacher plans to administer a speaking test to individual students. The **Lectures culturelles** section of the chapter is the best source for in-class reading. Selected activities in the **Vocabulaire** and **Structure** sections of each chapter are good sources for in-class writing assignments. The Workbook and Audio Activities booklet is an additional source.

Suggestions for Scoring the Speaking Tests

The following are suggestions to assist teachers in determining how to measure each student's response. Teachers may wish to place greater emphasis on the comprehensibility of the message conveyed than on grammatical accuracy. The following system is based on a scale of 1 to 5. For example:

5	(A):	Complete message conveyed, precise control of structure and vocabulary
4–3	(B–C):	Complete message conveyed, some errors in structure and vocabulary
2–1	(D):	Message partially conveyed, frequent errors
0	(F):	No message conveyed

Chapter Proficiency Tests

The Chapter Proficiency Tests measure mastery of vocabulary and grammar presented in each chapter on a more global, whole-language level. The Proficiency Tests can be used as an option to the Achievement Tests, or they may complement them. In order to minimize the total number of class days devoted to testing, the teacher may wish to combine several Chapter Proficiency Tests and administer them on the same day.

The Oral Proficiency Interview

Some years ago linguists in U.S. federal government service were asked to help develop a scale, a set of descriptors of speaking ability, and a procedure, a face-to-face interview, to determine proficiency level. A modified scale was later developed for use in the academic community. The modified scale is commonly known as the ACTFL (American Council on the Teaching of Foreign Languages) Proficiency Scale. The scales and interviews continue to be used by schools, colleges, government agencies, and increasingly by public and private institutions and agencies throughout the world for testing speaking proficiency in any language. The interview tests the ability to speak and to use the language in real-life situations.

The interview appears to be a casual conversation, but it is really more than that. A good interview will enable the student to produce a ratable sample of speech, one that is sufficiently complete and representative of the student's ability to allow for the assignment of a reliable rating.

The Oral Proficiency Interview is a proficiency test. That is, it is not based on a specific text, curriculum, or program of studies. Its purpose is to assess the ability of students to operate in real-life, face-to-face, language-use situations.

The Oral Proficiency Interview Scale

Novice

Novice Low	Unable to function in the spoken language
Novice Mid	Able to operate in only a very limited capacity
Novice High	Able to satisfy immediate needs with learned utterances

Intermediate

Intermediate Low	Able to satisfy basic survival needs and minimum courtesy requirements
Intermediate Mid	Able to satisfy some survival needs and some limited social demands
Intermediate High	Able to satisfy most survival needs and limited social demands

Advanced

Advanced	Able to satisfy the requirements of everyday situations and routine school and work assignments
Advanced High	Able to satisfy the requirements of a broad variety of everyday, school, and work situations
Superior	Able to speak the language with sufficient structural accuracy and vocabulary to participate effectively in most formal and informal conversations

Conducting the Oral Proficiency Interview

The interview consists of four phases: a warm-up, level checks, probes, and a wind-down.

1. The warm-up is intended to put the student at ease and consists of courtesies and very simple questions.
2. The level check is designed to verify that the student can perform at the level.
3. The probes are questions or stimuli at the level above the one at which the student has been responding. If the level check has verified that the student can perform at the Novice Mid level, for example, the probes should be at the Intermediate level.
4. The wind-down is the close of the interview. Once the interviewer is satisfied that the student has performed at the highest level possible, the interviewer "backs off," reduces the difficulty of the conversation so that the student can be comfortable, and ends the interview.

Length of the Interview and Target Performance

The length of the interview is directly related to the ability of the student. Novice level interviews will normally last five to eight minutes. A Superior level interview should require about twenty minutes. Students in the first year of study will typically rate in the Novice range. In the second year, performance in the Intermediate range should be expected. By the third year, students should be able to perform in the upper Intermediate range.

Level-Specific Tasks

What can the student do with the language? For each level there are tasks that the student must be able to perform. The focus is on successful completion of the task, not on grammatical perfection or precision of vocabulary. Obviously, for some high-level tasks, grammatical accuracy and precision of vocabulary are necessary to do the task. But at the Novice and Intermediate levels, all that is required is that the task be completed successfully.

Typical Novice Level Tasks

- label familiar objects
- repeat memorized material
- count

Typical Intermediate Level Tasks

- ask simple questions
- answer simple questions
- get into and out of survival situations

Typical Advanced Level Tasks

- give directions/instructions
- describe
- narrate in present, past, future

Typical Superior Level Tasks

- resolve problem situations
- support opinions
- hypothesize

A Note about "Situations"

The oral proficiency interview "situations" are designed to present the student with a task appropriate to his or her proficiency level. Intermediate level "situations," for example, are "survival" tasks such as obtaining lodging, ordering a meal, or asking for directions. For more information on "situations," please see the Introduction to the Situation Cards in this TeacherTools Fast File booklet.

Samples of Typical Interviewer Questions/Probes

The Warm-Up

Interviewer:	Salut. (Bonjour.) Ça va? (Comment vas-tu?) Je suis _____. (Je m'appelle _____.) Tu t'appelles comment? Il fait chaud (froid, frais) aujourd'hui, n'est-ce pas? Qui est ton professeur de français?

Level Check

Novice Level Interviewer:	Nous sommes quel jour aujourd'hui? Quelle est la date aujourd'hui? Quelle heure est-il? Qu'est-ce que c'est? (*articles of clothing/classroom objects/colors*) Quel temps fait-il aujourd'hui? Il y a combien de personnes dans ta famille? Qui sont les membres de ta famille?
Intermediate Level Interviewer:	Tu es d'où? Tu as quel âge? Parle-moi un peu de ta famille. Vous êtes combien? Quel âge ont les membres de ta famille? Est-ce qu'ils travaillent ou est-ce qu'ils sont élèves ou étudiants? Tu habites où? Comment est ta maison ou ton appartement? Tu es élève dans quel lycée? Tu suis

quels cours? Qu'est-ce que tu fais le matin (l'après-midi/le soir)? Tu pratiques quels sports? Comment est-ce qu'on va d'ici au centre-ville? Où est la cafétéria (le gymnase/le stade/ta maison/la poste)? Qu'est-ce que tu voudrais savoir à propos de moi? Qui sont tes amis? Ils ont quel âge? Ils sont comment? À quelle heure est-ce que tu te lèves? Qu'est-ce que tu manges au petit déjeuner (déjeuner/dîner)?

Situations:	Ordering meals/Exchanging money/Calling on the phone/Post office/Train or bus/ Lodging/Gas station
Advanced Level Interviewer:	Qu'est-ce que tu as fait samedi dernier? Tu es arrivé(e) comment au lycée ce matin? Quand tu étais petit(e), tu habitais où? Décris la ville où tu vivais, s'il te plaît. Je ne sais pas jouer au base-ball; explique-moi comment ça se joue. Qu'est-ce que tu vas faire cet après-midi après les cours? Parle-moi un peu du dernier film que tu as vu. Quelles qualités est-ce que tu cherches dans un bon ami? Quels sont tes projets d'avenir? Qu'est-ce que tu faisais à l'école primaire? Qu'est-ce que tu penses de ce qui se passe en/à (*current events topic*)? Explique-moi comment on se sert d'un(e) (*equipment/machine/gadget*)? Quand tu étais enfant, qui était ton meilleur ami (ta meilleure amie) et comment était-il/elle? Est-ce que tu as voyagé dans d'autres pays? Raconte-moi le voyage. Quelle est ton équipe de football favorite et pourquoi? Certaines personnes disent qu'on devrait avoir cours le samedi. Qu'est-ce que tu en penses? Pourquoi?
Situations:	Same as Intermediate Situations but with complications. For example: Ordering a meal, but can't find money/ Getting lodging, but only expensive rooms available/ Getting a train, but doesn't stop at desired station, etc.
Superior Level Interviewer:	Tu veux être avocat(e), n'est-ce pas? Alors, quelles qualités un(e) bon(ne) avocat(e) devrait-il/elle avoir? Qu'est-ce que tu ferais à propos de (*topical issue*) si tu étais Président des États-Unis? Beaucoup de gens croient que les études universitaires devraient être gratuites. Est-ce que c'est une bonne idée ou non? Pourquoi? Si tu avais un frère qui ne voulait pas étudier, qu'est-ce que tu lui dirais? Si tu étais le proviseur de ce lycée et si tu voyais un étudiant qui trichait pendant un examen, qu'est-ce que tu ferais?
Situations:	Convince a potential drop-out to stay in school/ Introduce the commencement speaker/Negotiate a good deal for team jackets/ Talk your French teacher into giving you a higher grade/ Talk your way out of a parking ticket in Paris.

The Wind-Down

| Interviewer: | Bien. Alors, est-ce que tu as des questions pour moi maintenant? Où vas-tu maintenant? Alors, je crois que c'est tout pour aujourd'hui. Merci, et à bientôt. |

The purpose of the wind-down is to put the candidate at ease and end the interview. It should be simple and easily understood.

The Oral Proficiency Interview: A Final Note

Remember that the preceding questions are only samples, indicative of the kinds of questions and topics appropriate at each level. The description we have given of the oral proficiency interview and scale will serve to familiarize the reader with a useful and respected tool for evaluating second-language oral proficiency. In order to administer and rate an interview properly, a thorough understanding of the scale and intensive training in interviewing and rating is usually necessary. For more information on oral proficiency interviews, write to:

The American Council on the Teaching of Foreign Languages (ACTFL)
6 Executive Plaza
Yonkers, NY 10701-6801

Nom _____ Date _____ ❖ _____

Reading and Writing Test

FORM A

(This test contains 40 items for convenience of scoring.)

Vocabulaire

 Identify each item.

1. _____

2. _____

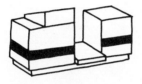

3. _____

4. _____

5. _____

6. _____

2 Answer each question based on the boarding pass.

```
┌──────────────────────────────────────┬─────────────────┐
│ ◄◄ ( 072 )  LEGRAND      NON FUMEURS  │ │ RETOUR: 01 AVR │
│                                       │ │                │
│ AIR FRANCE ///   EMBARQUEMENT         │ │    072         │
│ DE: NICE      À: BERLIN    BOARDING   │ │    05 A        │
│ 15 MARS BLN Y            1H30         │ │    902         │
│                         HEURE / TIME  │ │                │
│ AF 902   05 A    25                   │ │                │
│ VOL / FLIGHT  SIÈGE / SEAT PORTE/GATE │ │  AIR FRANCE // │
└──────────────────────────────────────┴─────────────────┘
```

1. Quel est le nom du passager?

_____

2. Quel est le numéro de son vol?

_____

3. Quelle est sa destination?

_____

4. Quel est le numéro de son siège?

_____

5. L'avion part à quelle heure?

_____

6. Il part de quelle porte?

_____

3 Choose the correct completion.

1. Un agent _____ le billet et le passeport au comptoir de la compagnie aérienne.
   a. achète   **b.** choisit   **c.** vérifie

2. L'avion atterrit sur _____.
   a. le hall   **b.** la piste   **c.** la cabine

3. Justine _____ une place côté couloir.
   a. choisit   **b.** fait   **c.** remplit

4. Pendant le vol le steward sert _____.
   a. des boissons   **b.** une carte de débarquement   **c.** une annonce

5. Il faut attacher _____ pendant le décollage et l'atterrissage.
   a. son écran   **b.** son siège   **c.** sa ceinture

6. Un vol _____ part et arrive dans le même pays.
   a. intérieur   **b.** international   **c.** en provenance d'une ville française

Structure

4 Complete each sentence with the correct form of the indicated verb.

1–4. Je suis à l'aéroport parce que je _____ (partir) pour le Canada. J'ai soif. Je vais au café de l'aéroport et je

_____ (choisir) un coca. Un serveur

_____ (servir) mon coca. Un autre passager

_____ (finir) sa boisson et va à la porte d'embarquement.

5–6. Nous _____ (choisir) nos sièges au comptoir de la

compagnie aérienne. Tu _____ (choisir) quel siège?

7–8. À la porte, je regarde les avions. Ils décollent ou ils

_____ (atterrir). Nous _____ (partir) dans vingt minutes.

9–10. À bord de l'avion, il y a beaucoup de passagers. Cinq ou six passagers

sont fatigués et ils _____ (dormir). Ton frère et toi,

vous _____ (remplir) votre carte de débarquement?

5 Complete each question with the correct form of **quel** and each response with the correct form of **tout.**

1–2. Agent 1: _____ bagages vont dans l'avion?

Agent 2: _____ les bagages!

3–4. Agent 1: _____ places sont occupées?

Agent 2: _____ les places!

5–6. Agent 1: Je vais enregistrer _____ valise?

Agent 2: Vous allez enregistrer _____ les valises!

7–8. Agent 1: _____ zone est non-fumeurs?

Agent 2: _____ l'avion est non-fumeurs.

Culture

6 Choose the correct completion.

1. La classe de Madame Cadet passe _____ en France.
   a. un bon weekend
   b. les vacances de Pâques
   c. tout le mois d'avril

2. Après un vol agréable, l'avion atterrit _____.
   a. au Mont-Saint-Michel
   b. à Charles-de-Gaulle à Roissy
   c. au centre de Paris

3. Après leur arrivée à l'aéroport, il faut passer par _____.
   a. le contrôle de sécurité
   b. la cabine de l'avion
   c. le contrôle des passeports et la douane

4. Les élèves de Madame Cadet prennent _____ qui fait la navette entre l'aéroport et Paris.
   a. le métro
   b. le taxi
   c. l'autocar

Nom _____ Date _____ ✤ _____

Reading and Writing Test

FORM B
(This test contains 30 items for convenience of scoring.)

Vocabulaire

1 Complete each sentence.

1–2. Maintenant Justine est dans le hall de l'aéroport.

Elle est au _____ où elle fait

_____ ses bagages.

3. Tous les passagers passent par _____ avant d'aller à

la porte d'embarquement.

4. Un avion atterrit et un autre _____.

5. À l'aéroport on peut voir les départs et les arrivées des vols sur un

_____.

6. L'avion n'arrive pas à l'heure. Il a du _____.

2 Answer each question.

1. Où faut-il mettre les bagages à main à bord de l'avion?

_____

2. Qu'est-ce qu'il faut attacher pendant le vol?

_____

3. Qu'est-ce que le steward sert à bord?

_____

Structure

3 Complete with the correct form of the indicated verb.

1. Il _____ son repas. (finir)

2. Les avions _____ sur les pistes. (atterrir)

3. Tu _____ une place côté fenêtre. (choisir)

4. Vous _____ une carte de débarquement avant
   d'arriver à votre destination? (remplir)

5. Je _____ un vol direct. (choisir)

4 Complete with the correct form of **tout** and **quel**.

1. _____ le personnel de cabine parle _____
   langues?

2. _____ les passagers remplissent _____ carte?

3. _____ les vols ont _____ destination?

4. _____ les places sont occupées sur _____ vol?

5 Rewrite each sentence.

1. Vous partez à quelle heure?

   Tu _____?

2. Il dort pendant le vol.

   Ils _____.

3. On sert un repas.

   Nous _____.

4. Ils sortent de la porte 5.

   Je _____.

Culture

6 Choose the correct sentence.

1. a. C'est le mois de juin et toute la classe de Madame Cadet va passer les vacances d'été en France.

b. C'est le mois d'avril et toute la classe de Madame Cadet va passer la semaine de Pâques en France.

2. a. Tous les élèves de Madame Cadet ont un passeport.

b. Les élèves de Madame Cadet n'ont pas de passeport.

3. a. Ils arrivent à Paris le soir.

b. Ils arrivent à Paris le matin.

4. a. Les taxis font la navette entre l'aéroport et le centre-ville.

b. Les autocars font la navette entre l'aéroport et le centre-ville.

7 Describe the illustration.

1–4. _____

_____

_____

_____

Chapitre 8

En option

(This test is optional and may be used with either the Form A or Form B Reading and Writing Test.)

Lecture supplémentaire 1

Answer each question.

1. Qu'est-ce que le décalage horaire?

_____

_____

2. Quand il est midi à New York, il est quelle heure à Paris?

_____

_____

Lecture supplémentaire 2

Give the following information.

1. Le nom d'un grand écrivain français

_____

2. La ville où il est né

_____

3. Sa profession

_____

4. Le titre d'un de ses livres

_____

5. Où cet auteur disparaît le 13 juillet, 1944

_____

Connexions: Le climat et le temps

Define each word.

1. le climat _____

_____

2. le temps _____

_____

Reading and Writing Tests
Answer Key

CHAPITRE 8

FORM A

1

1. un avion
2. un aéroport
3. un comptoir (de la compagnie aérienne)
4. une porte d'embarquement
5. une hôtesse de l'air
6. une ceinture de sécurité

2

1. Le nom du passager est Legrand.
2. Le numéro de son vol est AF 902.
3. Sa destination est Berlin.
4. Le numéro de son siège est 05 A.
5. L'avion part à 1 h 30.
6. Il part de la porte 25.

3

1. c	**4.** a
2. b	**5.** c
3. a	**6.** a

4

1–4. pars, choisis, sert, finit
5–6. choisissons, choisis
7–8. atterrissent, partons
9–10. dorment, remplissez

5

1–2. Quels, Tous	5–6. quelle, toutes
3–4. Quelles, Toutes	7–8. Quelle, Tout

6

1. b	**3.** c
2. b	**4.** c

FORM B

1

1–2. comptoir de la compagnie aérienne, enregistrer
3. le contrôle de sécurité
4. décolle
5. écran
6. retard

2

1. Il faut les mettre sous le siège ou dans le coffre à bagages.
2. Pendant le vol il faut attacher la ceinture de sécurité.
3. Le steward sert des boissons et un repas à bord.

3

1. finit	**4.** remplissez
2. atterrissent	**5.** choisis
3. choisis	

4

1. Tout, quelles	**3.** Tous, quelle
2. Tous, quelle	**4.** Toutes, quel

5

1. (Tu) pars à quelle heure?
2. (Ils) dorment pendant le vol.
3. (Nous) servons un repas.
4. (Je) sors de la porte 5.

6

1. b	**3.** b
2. a	**4.** b

7 *Answers will vary.*

En option

Lecture supplémentaire 1

1. Le décalage horaire est la différence entre l'heure d'une ville et l'heure d'une autre ville très loin.
2. Quand il est midi à New York, il est 18 h à Paris.

Lecture supplémentaire 2

1. Antoine de Saint-Exupéry est un grand écrivain français.
2. Il est né à Lyon.
3. Il est pilote.
4. Le titre d'un de ses livres est *Le Petit Prince.*
5. Il disparaît au-dessus de la mer Méditerranée.

Connexions

Answers will vary but may include:

1. Le climat est le temps qu'il fait chaque année dans la même région.
2. Le temps est la condition de l'atmosphère pendant une courte période.

Listening Comprehension Test

(This test contains 10 items for convenience of scoring.)

1 **1.** Compagnie aérienne: _____

2. Destination: _____

3. Numéro du vol: _____

4. Porte d'embarquement: _____

2

a. _____

b. _____

c. _____

d. _____

3 **1.**   a.   b.   c.

2.   a.   b.   c.

Listening Comprehension Test
Audio Script
CHAPITRE 8

Part 1

Item 1. Listen to the following announcement; then write the name of the airline on your answer sheet.

> Départ du vol Air France 176 à destination de Nice. Embarquement immédiat, porte 36.

Item 2. Listen to the announcement once more and now write the destination of the flight.

> Départ du vol Air France 176 à destination de Nice. Embarquement immédiat, porte 36.

Item 3. Listen once more and now write the flight number.

> Départ du vol Air France 176 à destination de Nice. Embarquement immédiat, porte 36.

Item 4. Listen for the last time and write the number of the departure gate.

> Départ du vol Air France 176 à destination de Nice. Embarquement immédiat, porte 36.

Part 2. You will hear four statements, each describing an illustration on your answer sheet. Write the number of the statement under the illustration it describes.

1. La passagère fait enregistrer ses bagages.
2. La passagère met ses bagages dans le coffre à bagages.
3. La passagère choisit sa place au comptoir de la compagnie aérienne.
4. La passagère a une place côté couloir.

Part 3. You will hear two questions each followed by three possible responses. Choose the appropriate response and circle **a, b,** or **c** on your answer sheet.

1. Que remplissent les passagers sur un vol international avant d'arriver à leur destination?
   a. Une porte d'embarquement.
   b. Une carte de débarquement.
   c. Un écran.

2. On annonce le départ de notre vol?
   a. Oui, on annonce le vol en provenance de Lyon.
   b. Oui, il faut vérifier le numéro de notre vol.
   c. Oui, il faut aller à la porte d'embarquement.

Answer Key
CHAPITRE 8

1
1. Air France
2. Nice
3. 176
4. 36

2
a. 2
b. 3
c. 4
d. 1

3
1. b
2. c

Nom _____ Date _____

Speaking Test

1 Look at the illustration. Say as much as you can about these airport activities.

Nom _____ Date _____

Proficiency Test

1 Write a paragraph about this illustration.

_____

_____

_____

_____

_____

_____

_____

2 Write some questions about the illustration.

_____

_____

_____

_____

_____

_____

_____

CHAPITRE

8

L'aéroport et l'avion

INTRODUCTION

The assessment materials provided here are part of the **Bon voyage!** Level 1 instructional program. These integrated, performance-based tasks are designed to provide the teacher with efficient alternatives for assessing language performance in the classroom.

For the teacher's convenience, each Performance Assessment Task is presented on a tear-out sheet that can be photocopied. The front side of each sheet contains "Notes to the Teacher" and includes a description of the Assessment Task and any special instructions for administering it. The Assessment Task itself appears on the reverse side and includes all the information the students need to carry out the activity. Only this reverse side, with spaces provided for **Nom** and **Date**, should be photocopied and distributed to the students.

Every chapter in **Bon voyage!** Level 1 has an Assessment Task. Of these fourteen Assessment Tasks, seven are designed to be done by students individually, and seven are designed for students working in pairs. The Assessment Tasks require from as little as five minutes of class time to as much as forty minutes. Several Assessment Tasks have directions in French; English directions are given in cases where the linguistic complexity of the directions in French would surpass the assumed reading level of first-year students or where directions in French would reveal important vocabulary or structures that the students are expected to supply independently when carrying out the task.

The teacher can select either the holistic or the analytic approach to scoring. For some tasks in which students both speak and write, the teacher can assign a score for each. A score can also be given on "cooperative learning" behavior or "group processes" for tasks in which pairs of students are required to work together.

How These Assessment Tasks Are Designed

Performance Assessments must include a number of important design features in order for the inferences made on a performance sample to be valid. For the purpose of assessment in the foreign language classroom, performance-based tasks need to imitate authentic communicative events; be linked to curricular goals; be representative of the relative emphasis placed on different types of activities in class; draw primarily on knowledge and skills students have had the opportunity to acquire during class; and be relevant and fair to diverse groups of students, male and female, of different ages and from different cultural and socioeconomic backgrounds.

The tasks match the instructional goals of the text.

These Assessment Tasks imitate the kinds of practice exercises found throughout the chapters in the textbook and incorporate only the knowledge, skills, and abilities covered up to that point in the textbook. Thus, students are not required to call on language skills they have not yet had the opportunity to acquire. Listening, speaking, reading, and writing are tested in varying degrees and combinations.

The tasks are relevant to the lifestyle of today's language student.

These Assessment Tasks require students to carry out activities that they would be likely to encounter if they lived in a French-speaking environment. There is enough variety in the tasks so that the teacher can select those that are best suited for the diversity of lifestyles, ages, and ability levels represented in the class. Some of the assessment activities require students to access and/or share new information with their classmates, creating an authentic context for communicating in French. "Information gap" activities are included to add authenticity to the information-sharing experience.

The tasks reflect current approaches to language teaching and learning.

The Assessment Tasks recognize not only the importance of linguistic competence but also discourse competence, sociolinguistic competence, and strategic competence; and they emphasize the "success of the message" in communication.

The tasks tap creativity and higher-order thinking.

While each Assessment Task requires knowledge and skills previously presented and practiced in the chapters of the textbook, the context for the performance required by a task will be new in some way, so that students can, to the extent possible, go beyond producing memorized material and use language creatively. To complete the tasks successfully, students are required to make inferences, analyze information, and solve problems.

Many of the tasks provide an opportunity to reinforce cooperative learning behaviors.

For the activities in which students are paired, it is recommended that the teacher observe the students as they work together and assign them a score for "cooperative learning" behavior.[1] Special rubrics, called the "Teacher Observation Checklist for Rating Group Processes," are provided for this purpose. The underlying assumption of this approach is that the second language learner needs to be conscious, not only of the language itself, but also of the social context of communication in that language. Scores can be given on the planning and sharing of work required by the task, participation, interaction, and communication. It is important that the teacher who chooses to give scores for "cooperative learning" during the assessments emphasize appropriate behavior in this regard regularly during class.

Incorporating the Assessment Tasks
Into the Language Program

It is suggested that the tasks be part of a "continuous assessment" program in which the teacher combines traditional quizzes and tests of grammar and vocabulary with several of these more integrated, performance-based activities to determine student progress. A printed and recorded "portfolio" of the completed tasks can be maintained for each student throughout the year. The written work can be collected and stored in a binder along with any recordings of the student's speaking tasks.

The Assessment Tasks are best administered at regular intervals during the semester when the students have completed the chapters indicated in "Notes to the Teacher." Throughout the course, the teacher may choose to use as many of these tasks as he or she wishes, depending on the extent to which the tasks coordinate with the language skills and practice activities emphasized in class, and the overall assessment objectives established in the curriculum. It is important to note that none of the tasks should be used as the sole criterion for determining a student's final grade or for making critical decisions about the student's future language education—for example, determining a student's readiness for entering or exiting a language program, awarding scholarships, and so on.

In order for these assessments to have a positive impact on student learning, the teacher should discuss the rating criteria (the scoring guides) with the students beforehand. As Herman et al. point out, ". . . discussions [of assessment criteria] help students to

---

[1] As different Assessment Tasks for pairs are administered throughout the semester, the students should be assigned to work together so that no student works with the same partner for more than one Assessment Task.

internalize the standards and 'rules' they need to become independent learners."[2] When communicating to the student his or her score, the teacher should use the descriptors in the guides to explain how the score was determined. It will be helpful to identify specific features in the student's speech or writing sample to explain to the student how the various aspects of his or her sample contributed to the resulting score. It is important, also, to refer to a score as a rating of the language sample collected on that particular task and not as a rating of the student's overall language proficiency.

How to Administer and Rate the Speaking Tasks

Tasks 3, 4, 6, 7, 8, 9, 10, 11, 12, 13, and 14 elicit a speech sample. For these tasks to "bring out the best" in student performance, the students should be familiar with the procedures for accomplishing these tasks and should have had the opportunity to speak individually in front of the class or in small groups at the discourse level, that is, more than one or two sentences at a time. It is recommended that the teacher rate tapes of the students' samples, rather than rating the speech "live," and that students be required to record their samples. A quiet area of the classroom or the school should be provided for the students to produce their samples. (The exceptions are Tasks 10 and 13, which are designed to be oral reports given in front of the class.)

Asking the students to produce their samples without recording them and rating them "live" during class may be less time-consuming, but it can be unreliable for several reasons. First, both the student and teacher can be distracted or influenced by the reaction of others in the class. Second, the responses of the students who perform first can influence the content of the responses of subsequent students. Third, if the teacher "misses" aspects of the performance, they cannot be recovered. Finally, with a score on a "live" performance only, the student has no evidence of the performance to which to relate the score he or she receives.

On the other hand, since a recorded speech sample provides evidence of proficiency that the student can hear for himself or herself, it can be a powerful instructional tool—the teacher can use a tape to point out to a student his or her particular strengths and weaknesses in spoken French. It can be more convenient to rate recordings because the teacher can decide when and where to do the scoring. The teacher can rewind a tape and listen to portions of the performance over again. The teacher also has the opportunity to check how consistently he or she is rating everyone in a class or in a number of classes by stopping halfway through the group of tapes and listening again to previously scored tapes.

The speaking tasks can be rated holistically using the "Holistic Scoring Guide for Rating Speaking and Writing Products" or analytically using the "Analytic Scoring Guide for Rating Speaking Products." For details, see the section "How to Use the Scoring Guides."

How to Administer and Rate the Writing Tasks

Tasks 1, 2, 4, 5, 7, 8, 10, 11, 12, and 13 elicit a writing sample. In several cases, the students can write their responses directly on the Assessment Task sheet. Suggested times are offered for each task, but it is assumed that the teacher will determine the time limit that is most appropriate for the level of the class. The use of dictionaries or the textbook during the in-class tasks is not recommended.

---

[2] Herman, J.L., Aschbachber, P.R., Winters, L. (1992), A Practical Guide to Alternative Assessment, The Regents of the University of California. Published by the Association for Supervision and Curriculum Development, 1250 N. Pitt St., Alexandria, VA 22314, p. 48.

Several samples should be rated in one sitting and the teacher should check how consistently he or she is rating students by stopping halfway through this procedure to reread previously scored samples. In scoring, the teacher should not make a point of counting errors, but rather should read to get an impression of the level of accuracy. The papers should not be marked up, because students may make incorrect inferences about the relationship between the number of markings and their scores. A portfolio can be collected for each student throughout the year to maintain evidence of student progress.

The writing tasks can be rated holistically using the "Holistic Scoring Guide for Rating Speaking and Writing Products" or analytically using the "Analytic Scoring Guide for Rating Writing Products." For details, see the following section, "How to Use the Scoring Guides."

How to Use the Scoring Guides

For the teacher's convenience, four types of rubrics, or scoring guides, are provided in this program: The "Holistic Scoring Guide for Rating Speaking and Writing Products," the "Analytic Scoring Guide for Rating Speaking Products," the "Analytic Scoring Guide for Rating Writing Products," and the "Observation Checklist for Rating Group Processes." Each scoring guide and hints for its use follow.

The "Holistic Scoring Guide for Rating Speaking and Writing Products"

The Holistic Scoring Guide requires the teacher to assign a single score based on the overall communicative quality of the language sample. In the descriptors, the "success of the message" communicated by the responses is evaluated on a four-point scale, accompanied by descriptions of proficiency in the use of the traditional language components of vocabulary, grammar, orthography, and pronunciation. By explaining the guide to students and using it regularly to score the performance tasks, the teacher will be reinforcing the value of "language as communication" for students. The holistic scores should be used in combination with the more traditional objective tests of grammar and vocabulary to collect a more integrative, comprehensive profile of a student's performance throughout the semester.

The Holistic Scoring Guide has been designed for easy use. To assign a rating to a writing or speech sample, the teacher should first decide how successful the sample is in communicating the important information required by the task. Then the teacher should consider the way the various language components, such as grammar, vocabulary, orthography, or pronunciation, contribute to the success of the message.

When reporting the score to the students, a 0 to 4 number score can be used. If the teacher wishes to discriminate more finely, points can be added to the scale in .5 increments. In other words, the intervals .5, 1.5, 2.5, and 3.5 can be added to the scale. The 0 to 4 score can be converted to an A, B, C, D, or F letter grade. The 0 to 4 score can also be converted to a percent scale. This can be done by multiplying the 0 to 4 score by .25. In this method, a 3 would be 75 percent on a scale of 100 percent.

The "Analytic Scoring Guide for Rating Speaking Products" and the "Analytic Scoring Guide for Rating Writing Products"

The Analytic Scoring Guides have been designed for the purpose of providing more detailed information about the various components of the student's speech or writing. (Note, however, that the analytic approach can be more complex and time-consuming than the holistic approach.) Each component (for example, vocabulary, grammar, message, pronunciation, mechanics) is treated equally in the rubrics. The various scores on the components can be reported separately or averaged together to come up with a final score from 0 to 4. Single component scores or average scores can be converted to a 100-percent scale by multiplying the total by .25.

   Depending on the teacher's assessment objectives for speaking and writing, components in the Analytic Scoring Guides can be de-emphasized or emphasized further by giving them differential weights in determining an overall percent score. For example, if one of the teacher's instructional objectives for writing has been to encourage students to take risks and to be more creative and he or she wishes to reflect this objective in the assessment, the teacher can de-emphasize grammatical accuracy and mechanics and give additional weight to the "message content" category. This can be accomplished by multiplying the vocabulary score by .25, the mechanics score by .20, the grammar score by .20, and the message content score by .35, adding the scores together and dividing by 4.

ANALYTIC SCORING GUIDE FOR RATING SPEAKING PRODUCTS

	VOCABULARY		GRAMMAR		PRONUNCIATION		MESSAGE CONTENT
4	Vocabulary is generally accurate and appropriate to the task; minor errors, hesitations, and circumlocutions may occur.	4	Grammar may contain some inaccuracies, but these do not negatively affect comprehensibility.	4	Completely or almost completely comprehensible; pronunciation errors, rhythm and/or intonation problems do not create misunderstandings.	4	Relevant, informative response to the task. Adequate level of detail and creativity.
3	Vocabulary is usually accurate; errors, hesitations, and circumlocutions may be frequent.	3	Some grammatical inaccuracies may affect comprehensibility; some control of major patterns.	3	Generally comprehensible, but pronunciation errors, rhythm and/or intonation problems may create misunderstandings.	3	Response to the task is generally informative; may lack some detail and/or creativity.
2	Vocabulary is not extensive enough for the task; inaccuracies or repetition may be frequent; may use English words.	2	Many grammatical inaccuracies may affect comprehensibility; little control of major patterns.	2	Difficult to comprehend because of numerous pronunciation errors, rhythm, and intonation problems.	2	Response incomplete; lacks some important information.
1	Vocabulary inadequate for most basic aspects of the task.	1	Almost all grammatical patterns inaccurate, except for a few memorized patterns.	1	Practically incomprehensible.	1	Response not informative; provides little or no information.
0	No response.	0	No response.	0	No response.	0	No response.

ANALYTIC SCORING GUIDE FOR RATING WRITING PRODUCTS

	VOCABULARY		GRAMMAR		MECHANICS		MESSAGE CONTENT
4	Vocabulary is generally accurate and appropriate to the task; minor errors may occur.	4	Grammar may contain some inaccuracies, but these do not negatively affect comprehensibility.	4	Good control of the mechanics of French; may contain occasional errors in spelling, diacritics, or punctuation, but these do not affect comprehensibility.	4	Relevant, informative response to the task. Adequate level of detail and creativity.
3	Vocabulary is usually accurate; occasional inaccuracies may occur.	3	Some grammatical inaccuracies may affect comprehensibility; some control of major patterns.	3	Some control of the mechanics of French; contains errors in spelling, diacritics, or punctuation that sometimes affect comprehensibility.	3	Response to the task is generally informative; may lack some detail and/or creativity.
2	Vocabulary is not extensive enough for the task; inaccuracies may be frequent; may use English words.	2	Many grammatical inaccuracies may affect comprehensibility; little control of major patterns.	2	Weak control of the mechanics of French; contains numerous errors in spelling, diacritics, or punctuation that seriously affect comprehensibility.	2	Response incomplete; lacks some important information.
1	Vocabulary inadequate for most basic aspects of the task.	1	Almost all grammatical patterns inaccurate, except for a few memorized patterns.	1	Almost no control of the mechanics of French.	1	Response not informative; provides little or no information.
0	No response.	0	No response.	0	No response.	0	No response.

The "Observation Checklist for Rating Group Processes"

The Observation Checklist is for use in observing the student pairs as they carry out Tasks 4, 7, 10, 11, 12, 13, and 14 and is most appropriately used in a language program that regularly places emphasis on the social context of communication and learning. Underlying such emphasis is the recognition that in second language acquisition the learner needs to be receptive both to those with whom he or she is communicating and to the language itself, be responsive to persons and to the context of communication, and value interpersonal exchange. Such a language program would provide numerous opportunities for students to work in pairs and groups to accomplish a common task, take on a variety of roles, and develop the necessary skills for collaborating successfully with others. In such a program, using the Observation Checklist as well as the Holistic or Analytic Scoring Guides would link assessment to these special behavioral goals.

The extent to which the assessment of group processes influences the students' scores on the Assessment Tasks is for the teacher to decide. The Checklist describes three basic categories of cooperative behavior with three levels in each category. Numbers were not assigned to these levels in order to avoid confusion with the numbers associated with the Holistic and Analytic Rubrics. The teacher can choose to use these descriptors as they stand or assign his or her own alphabetical or numerical grading system to them, depending upon his or her teaching objectives in a given domain and the behavioral characteristics of a particular class. This Checklist is also useful for informally assessing student processes during regular group activities.

OBSERVATION CHECKLIST FOR RATING GROUP PROCESSES
(Teacher selects one description in each category while observing each group)

PLANNING AND SHARING THE GROUP'S WORK	MEMBER PARTICIPATION	GROUP INTERACTION AND COMMUNICATION
Almost equal distribution of planning and work between partners.	Both partners participate equally, share responsibility for task.	Active listening, lively discussion and interaction by both partners.
Both partners contribute to planning and problem solving; some sharing of work.	Both partners participate at some point and contribute something to the task.	Some discussion of ideas and some active listening by both partners.
Strong reliance on one partner to plan/organize and carry out the task.	Only one partner actively participates; the other may be disinterested or distracted.	Very little or sporadic conversation; some conversation not on task.

Notes to the Teacher

Task 8   FAIRE UN VOYAGE

This assessment task incorporates the narrating function, in which events are described in chronological order, and vocabulary related to air travel. Students will most likely use the present tense to relate their stories. In formulating a successful response, they are likely to use vocabulary related to airplane travel and third person singular and plural verbs. (Students will not have learned adverbials such as **d'abord** or **ensuite,** but will be able to use the vocabulary learned in Chapter 8 to tell what is occurring in each picture.)

Use the "Holistic Scoring Guide for Rating Speaking and Writing Products" to evaluate the students' responses in either the speaking or writing task. Use the "Analytic Scoring Guide for Rating Speaking Products" or the "Analytic Scoring Guide for Rating Writing Products" if you prefer a more detailed evaluation.

TIME REQUIRED: Ten to fifteen minutes of supervised class time for a speaking task; fifteen to twenty minutes of supervised class time for a writing task

SPECIAL MATERIALS REQUIRED: An audiocassette player or videocassette recorder

Nom _____ Date _____

Task 8   FAIRE UN VOYAGE

DIRECTIONS FOR A SPEAKING TASK

Anne et son frère Michel partent pour Dakar en avion. Décris *(Describe)* leurs activités oralement. Utilise les dessins comme guide. Tu as cinq minutes pour préparer ta réponse; tu peux prendre des notes *(take notes)*. Ensuite *(Then)*, parle pendant trente secondes.

DIRECTIONS FOR A WRITING TASK

Anne et son frère Michel partent pour Dakar en avion. Décris *(Describe)* leurs activités dans un paragraphe. Utilise les dessins comme guide. Écris une ou deux phrases pour chaque *(each)* dessin. Tu as quinze minutes pour écrire ton paragraphe.